CHAIN LETTER

To: You

CHAIN LETTER

written by Lucille Lang Day

illustrated by Doug Dworkin

Heyday Books

Berkeley, California

Heyday Books, founded in 1974, works to deepen people's understanding and appreciation of the cultural, artistic, historic, and natural resources of California and the American West. It operates under a 501(c)(3) nonprofit educational organization (Heyday Institute) and, in addition to publishing books, sponsors a wide range of programs, outreach, and events.

To help support Heyday or to learn more about us, visit our website at www.heydaybooks.com, or write to us at P.O. Box 9145, Berkeley, CA, 94709.

Library of Congress Cataloging-in-Publication Data
Day, Lucille.
Chain letter / by Lucille Lang Day ; illustrated by Doug Dworkin.
p. cm.
ISBN 1-59714-011-2 (hardcover : alk. paper)
1. Letter writing—Juvenile poetry. 2. Letters—Juvenile poetry. 3. Children's poetry, American. I. Dworkin, Doug, 1968- ill. II. Title.
PS3554.A965C47 2005
811'.54--dc22
2005006192

Book design by Rebecca LeGates

Orders, inquiries, and correspondence should be addressed to:
Heyday Books
P. O. Box 9145, Berkeley, CA 94709
(510) 549-3564, Fax (510) 549-1889
www.heydaybooks.com

Printed in Thailand by Imago

10 9 8 7 6 5 4 3 2 1

For my grandchildren, Brandon and Sabine—L.L.D.

For Suzanne, Joanne, and William, without whom these illustrations would have been impossible—D.D.

To: You

This letter is for good luck.
It has been around the world
nine times in a bottle.

The original is buried in a time capsule underneath the Tower of London.

You will receive good luck within four days. This is no joke.

All you need to do is send out 10,000 copies within 24 hours.

The Chain comes from the Galápagos.
Charles Darwin brought it back with him
on the H.M.S. Beagle.

HMS
MAIL

Do not ignore the following: in 1992 Rafael Raincoat received this letter...

...and asked his secretary to make 10,000 copies and send them out.

MAIL ROOM
MAIL
MAIL
The Statue of Liberty saw this

and gave him
12 million dollars.

oakley Funk received the chain,
did not believe in it,
and threw it away.

A rattlesnake rose from the toilet and bit him.

A young woman in California put it aside to do later.

An elephant sat on her car,

so she found the letter and sent it out.

She won a stretch limousine.

ANNUAL ELEPHANT
SHOW
WINNER
ANT
OW

You must start sending out copies immediately. In a few days you will get a pleasant surprise.

If you break the chain,
the Abominable Snowman
will arrive by noon next Friday
to take you away.

Remember
a•bom•i•na•ble
ə-bŏm′-ə-nə-bəl
YAK
UNCH
To Do:
FOOD

This will happen even if you are not superstitious.

Remember me always.
With love
all things are possible.
To: You

Special Delivery
To: You

HMS